Leslie Wood
Sam's Big Day

Oxford University Press

Oxford Toronto Melbourne

Sam works in the shunting yard

But one day up ran the
station master.

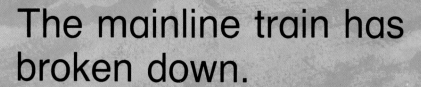

The mainline train has broken down.

Sam hitched up. . .

. . .and off they went.

Hurrying past fields and hills

and cows and sheep.

To the big city.

And not a minute late!
Well done Sam!

But it was all a dream.

Oxford University Press, Walton Street, Oxford OX2 6DP

Oxford is a trade mark of Oxford University Press

© Leslie Wood 1987
First published 1987

British Library Cataloguing in Publication Data
Wood Leslie
Sam's big day. — (Cat on the mat)
I. Title   II. Series
823'.914 [J]   PZ7
Printed in Hong Kong